Beauty & Ashes

Beauty & Ashes

Poems by

Karen Warinsky

© 2025 Karen Warinsky. All rights reserved.
This material may not be reproduced in any form, published,
reprinted, recorded, performed, broadcast,
rewritten, or redistributed without
the explicit permission of Karen Warinsky.
All such actions are strictly prohibited by law.

Cover design by Shay Culligan
Cover image by Karen Warinsky
Author photo by Mariah Plantier

ISBN: 978-1-63980-727-7
Library of Congress Control Number: 2025935599

Kelsay Books
502 South 1040 East, A-119
American Fork, Utah 84003
Kelsaybooks.com

"I can be changed by what happens to me.
But I refuse to be reduced by it."
—Maya Angelou

The title of this book is inspired in part from a Bible passage, Isaiah 61:3 which states ". . . to bestow on them a crown of beauty instead of ashes, the oil of joy instead of mourning, and a garment of praise instead of a spirit of despair."

Sometimes life has turned things around for me so that I received "beauty instead of ashes," or "beauty from ashes" as some put it, but really, like everyone, I live with beauty *and* ashes. The poems in this book take the reader through the seasons of the year in both moments of satisfaction and moments of questioning and despair. We must learn to reckon with it all.

Karen Warinsky

Acknowledgments

The author wishes to acknowledge the editors of the publications and online sites where the following poems first appeared:

2024 National & International Goddess Anthology, Honoring Women: "Cellophane"
Ain't No Dead Beats Around Here: "Revival"
Baseball Bards: "Little League Moms"
The Ekphrastic Poetry Trust: "Mirage" (First Place Winner)
GAS: Poetry, Art & Music: "Believer," "The Burning of Old Love," "Real Heart," "Swimming in the Time of Kali Yuga"
Halfway Down the Stairs: "Rite of Spring"
Joy Interrupted, an anthology of motherhood and loss: "Departure for College"
Light Magazine: "The Orange Tunnel"
The Lothlorien Poetry Journal: "Precipice," "Toward the Horizon"
The Naugatuck Review: "Bellerophon's Downfall"
The New Verse News: "Favorite Goddess," "O Holy Night," "Searching," "From the Dark"
Orenaug Mountain Poetry Journal: "Like Condensed Milk," "Winter Poem," "Solstice Moon"
The Rambler: "Sunset on Mars" "Watching Animal Rescue Videos"
The Rye Whiskey Review: "Tonight Is a Poem," "Sunday at Rusty's," "Watching Falling Leaves While Drinking Coffee in My Car," "Gratitude"
Silkworm: "A Folder for Death," "Summer Dross"
Worcester Magazine: "Mercy," "The Loudest Voice"
Wordpeace: "One Love," "Asymmetry," "Brought Back"

Contents

SUMMER

A Greeting	17
Morning Glories & Lace	18
Holier	19
Say Yellow	20
One Love	21
Believer	22
Tonight Is a Poem	23
Elegy for Pearl	24
Carillon	26
Swimming in the Time of Kali Yuga	28
New Category	29
Like Condensed Milk	31
Mirage	32
Every Night in Egypt	33
Summer Dross	34

FALL

Orange Tunnel	37
Departure for College	38
This Ruined Garden	40
If They Say They Are	42
I Am the Chief	43
Keeping Summer	45
Watching Falling Leaves While Drinking Coffee in My Car	46
Pinter Play	47
A Folder for Death	48
Precipice	49
Sunset on Mars	51

Screaming at the Guy at the Transfer Station	52
The Loudest Voice	54
Flags Waving	56
Compounding Disasters	57
Facebook Buddha/Empty Bowl	58
Subtle Things	60
Whatever Comes	61
The Phone Rang	62

W I N T E R

Winter Poems	65
Snow Globe	66
Solstice Moon	67
Bear	68
Favorite Goddess	69
Tombs	70
Cellophane	72
Asymmetry	73
O Holy Night	74
The Tide	75
Weather Report	76
Sunday at Rusty's	77
Bellerophon's Downfall	78
The Burning of Old Love	80
Guess You Forgot	81
February Sun	82
This View	83
From the Dark	84
Reclamation	85
The Idea of It	86
Toward the Horizon	87

S P R I N G

Rite of Spring	91
Dream in March	92
Little League Moms	93
Future Perfect	94
Intention	95
Gratitude	96
Your MG	97
When I Think of Utah	98
Moonlight Becomes Her	99
If You Were Mine	101
Real Heart	102
Honorable Mention	103
Dent-de-Lion	104
Searching	105
Mercy	107
Watching Animal Rescue Videos	108
Nothing Left but to Be a Shaman	110
A Burst of Sunshine	112

*

SUMMER

A Greeting

Summer, my love
I succumb to your sunshine bursts
arms of warmth wrapping me gently
my feet soaking up your hellos
from the smooth stone path around my house.

Energy swirled
inside your golden sphere
for millions of years
before its eight-minute trip
finding me,
a faded gray popsicle
a tired woolen sweater
a woman of last nerve,
thawed me
said,
"Kick off those shoes and dance!
Solstice is here."

Morning Glories & Lace

Two morning glories sit among the weeds
five-sided delicates
lilac and white swaying on a rib of green.
Do they sense their simple elegance
as a young girl discerns admiring eyes upon her,
instinct of beauty seeping into consciousness?
Or are they only aware of the breeze
the bugs and the sun
whose mighty absence shuts their faces into folds,
shadow forcing them to rest and dream of dawn?

Queen Anne's Lace is also there
a flower ballet, all adagio,
a positioned, patterned perfection.
I touch its holy white head
joining nature,
giving another nod to the Great God who tolerates me.

Holier

Nothing holier than a cornfield,
stalks spire straight
make their green announcement of heaven above;
quiet sanctuary for children in summer
when the field's heart becomes a hidden fort
protecting wishes whispered on mashed green leaves.

Nothing lovelier than a patch of morning glories,
tissue paper faces gently wafting
white and lavender
deep and mysterious
shutting into a tight twist of silk in the afternoon shade.

Nothing quicker than the chipmunk,
monk that he is
scurrying over a stone wall
seeking privacy and solace.

Nothing finer than a baby's little fingers,
or a smile from someone
who hated you yesterday.

Say Yellow

Say buttercup
      say glow
            say sunflower
                  say saffron
                        say sandy beach
                              brushed, blonde hair
                                    shine,
                                          sunshine.

Say you're mostly happy on an amber day
gold vibrating around all things
feeling easy in a citrine cast
forgetting

it's the color of caution.

One Love

Maybe it was from those Marley vibes infusing the air
all of us dancing and hopping around
after so long without live music,
or the fact that I was a beer and two shots in
that kept my face in place
when a man turned to tell me
he once stabbed a guy 15 times
over stolen money, then asked,

"Have you ever been to Providence?"

Guess I've just heard too much
seen too much
awash in daily bombings on TV
gunfire on all channels
privy to too many strange, sad stories
because I didn't flinch
just listened,
played confessor,
then danced away.

Now, another mass shooting
this term unknown to me as a girl
and I wonder what providence we have left
here in this dream country,
this place so many still struggle to enter,
this "last best hope of earth."

Believer

Now that I love myself
fully
to the max
there's no one good enough
no one I'd rather wait for
at a sidewalk café,
stumble into at a restaurant, a store,
no one better than me to run an idea by,
take out for a treat,
offer half of my donut to
(maybe I'll just save it for tomorrow)
write a poem for.

Wish, oh wish I'd had this true love
of self
all those years ago
when I pinned so much on you,
gave you the cream, the first bite, the biggest slice,
waited quiet, silent, for the yes
as you put your lips around all that was offered,
indulged yourself at my banquet,
watched for
the nod, the smile that said
you would grant your time, your breath,
for a bit
before saying
it was time for me to go home.

Tonight Is a Poem

Because we're here
feeling good
safe for the moment
money in our pockets
beer on the table
breathing in
breathing out
smiling in your eyes
hugging when I can
brushing up to let you know
the caring is killing me
and there's nothing I can do
except feel all this
love
desire this
friendship
hope it stays intact.
Forget tomorrow
her suitcase of problems
and her trippy drippy doubts
because
tonight
is a poem
and I want it
to write all over me.

Elegy for Pearl

Almost wish I hadn't seen her, just kept my blurry vision
bequeathed from Dad's childhood tales,
sepia memories.

Years ago, a thousand souls lived there
pulling mussels from the Illinois River, chipping the shells
cutting out that rainbow shine for shirt buttons
finished off at the factory in Meredosia.
Others worked the quarry or farmed small plots
inherited from European predecessors,
folks who found their way into the new country's beating heart
when the Old World bled out.

Great Grandma took in wash, sewed,
got a mother's pension,
raised the children left to her
the day he put the rope around his own neck
his reasons buried with him in Green Pond Cemetery.
She grew her garden, canned, made do,
had her life along the river;
friends in town, gossip at the grocery,
prayer and penance at church.

A ferry still takes travelers across the muddy expanse
drops them off on Pearl's shoulder
but no buttons are made
no stores remain in Utnapishtim's mirror,
empty buildings shouting "Keep Out!" from spray painted mouths.

A lone cat wandered among the abandoned houses
picked his way through debris, wet clothing, forgotten toys.
Porcelain fixtures lay in the grass like headstones
and the whole place felt like a grave,
abandoned meth labs behind rotting doors,
a Zombie Apocalypse aftermath.

Great Grandma's house is there amid the ruin.
I picked some violets from the yard,
took them to the cemetery
laid them on her stone, whispered,
"We remember you."

Carillon

The fanciest word I knew as a child was "carillon,"
three syllables of embodied melody
and my mother would say it
as if she'd known it all her life
but it wasn't true
because she said "ain't" and "git" and "fer"
same as all the moms from the south,
and she didn't know about Alfonso the Wise
or 13th-century Flanders
where the instrument was created,
though she had been out to California
when she was a child,
and even took a trip to Ohio once
to see her sister.

She learned it at church
when the handsome preacher explained
how they needed to finish
raising money to buy one,
a carillon,
beautiful bells
that would play the first two
verses of hymns at noon and at 5 o'clock.

Sometimes at noon we ignored
the lilting sounds,
but at 5 o'clock
it was a signal
a warning to come home
supper cooking
Dads returning from their day's work
expectant of small, smiling faces and a hot meal,
though we children didn't rush back till
the last note of the last verse
had chimed.

Swimming in the Time of Kali Yuga

Her fears sometimes glide inside me
doing butterfly kicks and easy breast strokes
while I cannot swim.
My fear of water runs deep
placed there by my mother's stories and doubts,
a liquid fright running over every part of her life
doused by the 20th century,
the opening act of the apocalypse,
the Kali Yuga, the singularity.

It was windy and cool
the morning of our diving lessons
and the young teacher
kept her clothes on over her swim suit,
so I thought,
"She won't come in after me."
"She won't get her clothes wet,"
because I had been dipped in doubt,
prepared for betrayal,
taught to expect the worst.

I stopped taking lessons.

Years later my three children became lifeguards;
strong and fearless they dove
swam past the buoys
saved others
an overcompensation for my driftwood life
which had taken me far from my past
from many worries,
though I am always watching for
a flash flood,
a time of unexpected inundation,
a time when nature decides to take back what is hers.

New Category

Ok, Nora Ephron, you were right,
it's the chicken neck that is the worst
but the backs of the hands
when held a certain way
also show
the long years lived.

Too busy during the other categories
(45–50, 50–55, 55–60)
filling out forms at the doctor's office
re-financing the mortgage
caring for elders
holding down the job, the house,
floating the children out into the world
to dwell on the progression
though I did throw myself a party at 60;
a milestone and me still upright
ready for a good time.
We took over the upper floor of Waterfront Mary's,
had an open bar, food, a DJ
and danced like the crazies we are.
But now it's here: "65 and up,"
and though I get half off the transfer station permit
a reduced rate at museums and ten cents off
a small hot coffee
it's not the thrill I'd hoped for
and "the up" part gives me pause.

Still, I could have a way to go as I just learned
the oldest person in the world passed at 118;
a French nun, and yes,
I'm about as far from a French nun as you can get
however, I will follow her lead
have a daily glass of red wine, a bite of chocolate
do some good works,

keep my hands warm and open,
held out for a friendly shake or a desperate grasp,
ready to help all who dare enter
this new category with me.

Like Condensed Milk

An analepsis flashes before me
scenes of your life once so deeply twined with mine,
days when nothing happened to me without you
and nothing happened to you without me,
and we weren't "one" but your little hugs and graces
your distorted drawings and cards saying
"For Mom"
decorated the fridge, the bedroom mirror,
so plentiful I could send some to relatives and friends,
nothing missed in the sparing.

This year you will marry
and time is now condensed milk,
a thick syrupy concoction
all excess boiled away,
sugar added, sweetening all things
even loss,
and the pictures of your young life
crash and flash before me
and it's true what they say
how it all collapses into a moment
when looking back,
the hours a vapor,
the days a dream.

Mirage

No motors
only the lap of the lip of water
kissing ancient rock in a spring-fed pond
a favorite spot of Nipmucks, Mohegans,
Pequots, Naragansetts,
now a town swimming hole
frequented by colonial progeny.

Boulders of ochre and rust
beige and brown
turn into Egyptian pyramids in hazy afternoons
appearing to rise from the clean, cool Nile
as I float in my kayak
dreaming of Karnak, Luxor, Alexandria.

Every Night in Egypt

The camels walk in blasé pace
find a place to sit, day's work done.

The earth turns again
losing the sun one color at a time—
ombré of ochre, green, red, blue
blazing behind the pyramids, the statues
before making way for the night goddess and her shawl of stars.

Nuit, are you happy with you lot?
Lonely sky goddess you are forgotten
as we, seated, our eyes on screens
or drinking in well-lit establishments
busy ourselves with life in the New World.

But there you go each night swallowing the sun,
finding your husband again,
god of the earth,
spend a few hours together till the next day
when you must birth that hot star back into existence
and he must rule all that lives and grows,
you dear queen, protecting his efforts.

Today, a man and wife rush out
leave their house behind,
hop in cars, drive to jobs
thoughts on the tasks before them,
separated by distance yet aiming together
bound by goals till they return home
and sometimes watch the sunset.

Summer Dross

I pull death from the plants,
fresh green revealed under what's expired;
short summer life.

Daylilies, June's pleasure
shot and slimy in two weeks,
some hanging on as their siblings wilt in July heat
despite watering and pep talks,
despite my need to bask in summer.

I scrape death out of the corner of the driveway
leathery leaves mustering,
blown in from the hill where foliage mulches in all seasons
a tawny, spongy brown on the ground;
scrape it out of crooks in the stonewall,
yank it from between clusters of Pachysandra,
my yearly vigil to release what's verdant
what's thriving,
yeoman's work here on my little forested plot.

It feels like a win
though winds will blow it back
and weeds will entwine with this litterfall,
so, I step back,
concentrate on all that's alive
all that blooms, shines, glistens,
all that screams of Now.

* F A L L

Orange Tunnel

So, I'm flying through the orange tunnel
feeling the relief that comes after a long day of work,
paying attention to the details;
light, color, shadows
the song on the radio
the barn in the field
the bird on the wire and
the cat in the weeds with its ability to balance
and its desire to hide.

Paying attention to the inside.

All here before, this nature
but lately it's soaked into my mind,
protection against the cold grey file cabinets
the rust-chipped, mottled metal desks
with the fake, fraying wood trim
ripping away around the edges,
the harshness of others, their boredom
and the lack of caring they tend to display.

Time flies with me in the orange tunnel as I absorb
the splash of saffron on the leaves of those thick bushes,
observe the deep maroon cascade of wet, waxy ivy
pushing out from the center of trees
that will stand and stand
and not fall down
till I'm gone,
and I roll down the window and feel the air,
letting it come in and blow my hair into a mess,
try to find my freedom in this moment
passing through and reaching out to this beautiful,
marigold tunnel of leaves.

Departure for College

They are departing, to Baltimore,
to Denver,
to a college in Florida.

The last few weeks
spent in a nightly clench
of "good times,"
secret wine and
sleep outs, night walks.

The cell phones have messaged in a flow of checking in
and arranging to get there,
to be together to have one last cup of coffee,
one last swim,
one last chat.
They know this time is ending and it scares them.

It infuriates the one left behind.

Community College was not part of her plan.
She feels cheated, betrayed, foiled.
She doesn't care about finances, or reasons why,
or apologies from weary parents.
A year is not a *SHORT TIME*.
All offers to *MAKE IT BETTER*
with train trips or plane trips or laptops
go unheard.
She is a red, angry sore,
hot to touch
wanting no touching.
No hugging.
No kiss on the cheek from Betrayers.

The mother remembers another day . . .
two children
recent acquaintances
a boy and a girl
both five (so wonderful to be five),
one tousle-headed,
one pig-tailed.

Through the window she saw them
running together on the hill by the house,
streaming through the trees,
fairy feet on dry leaves.
Building a "fort."

Later, they were laughing on the top bunk,
laughing like they had always known each other,
these small, elfin children.
It was a perfect moment.
A perfect friendship,
and she saw.

This Ruined Garden

Some are oblivious by choice, or youth, or age.
Some lock their hearts and shutter their eyes
no longer bearing to look at all that has happened,
is happening.
Successfully shielded with denial and medication
they focus on the minutia of life—
coffee too hot,
weather too chill,
dissect their distractions;
celebrity,
fashion,
passion.

We have our garden; a good idea in May
when summer's anticipation swells every living thing,
the dirt's promised abundance seductive.
Perdurable winter and the muddy, wet spring
make digging, planting, growing,
seem a noble participation
though the end product is not enough to fill a table
just a couple bowlfuls of tomatoes
a colander of green beans
some rhubarb that will never make it to a pie;
a hobby, not a vocation.

But now, as fall begins and we tumble into the year's end
I poke around in this ruined garden,
shuffle through its tangled plants and fibers
that didn't add a thing, really, to our lives
just another half-hearted distraction from a troubled world,
a world fallen thousands of years before
a world that disappoints and rescues
fascinates and terrifies
a world that each spring brings us a promise
we cannot refuse.

If They Say They Are

When someone posts a sign that says,
"The Witch is In," believe them.

A few years ago, I did battle with a witch. At least she declared herself so, and all of us working in the department came to know this truth.

But I needed the job, so I danced around her rude remarks, her frightening, sudden, scowling appearances at my classroom door, her disinterest whenever I tried some friendly conversation, her outright lies about my personality and my job performance.

It was getting to me and so I tried some witch magic back; white magic. Posted beautiful mandalas on the wall between our rooms filling my eyes with the colors and patterns, sending positive energy my way, blocking her blackness out. Gave her sincere compliments whenever I could. Sought her advice. Tried to lay low.

She won many battles, never answering my honest question:
"How can we get along better?"
Looked shocked when I said I wanted to improve our relationship.

But I may have won the war because I kept it steady, kept it friendly on my end, kept my job.
Paid the bills.

I Am the Chief

I made it.

Through the day, through the leaves, through the chill,
(the one from colleagues and the one from Mother N.)
through lunch alone
and all those kids in my classroom
and all those kids in the halls
passing me as I stand at my station
gearing up for another round.

But there was Anna, (my favorite), and London, the hugger,
Bialik who likes to make strange noises with me,
and Mia who drives me crazy and Courtney
(which one you ask?)
who had a schedule change after two weeks
but has been like an appendage since then
shouting "Chief!" at least twice a day,
and all the other kids from the past few years
who somehow attached themselves to me,
decided I was alright.
We help each other through our days.

I'll be trying to lead the lesson
keep everyone engaged and enthralled
when someone from the hall will stop and shout into my room:

"Chief!"
"Chieftain!"

A warning look is sent if it's the wrong moment to visit
(DO NOT COME IN HERE!)
but if things are done, daily goals achieved,
I will wave and smile and sometimes let them in
to tell their tale, lead the vocab quiz
or reminisce about their good times in last year's class.

I get it.

That's why they like me.

They love me, actually.

That's why I'm the Chief.

Keeping Summer

Yes, yes, it's the first day of fall
but I am not rushing to put out pumpkins
slap a leafy orange garland around my door,
drink pumpkin ale.

Why the hurry?
The recollective cold and dreary dark days are coming.
Can't we just use our sense and will power
to keep the fawns
the green soft grass
the shoeless, fleece-less summer
one month more?

I'll willingly kill the mosquitos
sweep up those prompt, premature fallen leaves
from the steps
the deck
the end of the driveway
and brush them off my geraniums
my potted ivy
just to see sweet Sol's face
shining back at me, his loyalist lover.

I want my windows open
my ceiling fan turning, humming its quiet refrain
restraining me from worry
from fear
keeping the mood light,
the summer sunset in the sky.

Watching Falling Leaves While Drinking Coffee in My Car

Can't get enough
of the crazy colors,
the deep hues
that suddenly shock
to pale and neon yellows and greens,
all that amber and peach litterfall
dead quiet on the ground
waiting to mulch;
absorb the silent lesson.

But I hadn't been out all day
so, drove to the bank, got gas,
then the drive-through for
coffee and (yes) a donut.
Went to a favorite parking lot near a brook
where the trees are screaming
in orange, pink, maroon,
refusing to go quietly,
and watched one by one
the abscission,
the cutting off as the branches pinch closed,
the trees firmly deciding
they will live another year
pushing out what's done,
like an expired friendship,
a dead love.

Pinter Play

It has become a Pinter Play.

A man and a woman sit at a table
eating a meal
talking about a broken lamp
the cat
the cold.

Our house is nice, tidy and comforting
but the rooms echo memories and something is missing.

The cast is missing.

I still call it "the girls' room."
"It's in the girls' room" I say,
before correcting and saying, "the office."
It's only been an office for six months.
Guess I will get used to it.
The other room
that housed each child at a point in their life
is now the "little bedroom."
Somehow that is easier to say.

Meanwhile the dialogue stays sparse
we sit at the table, or down in the family room
pet the cats
comment on the weather, our day,
look for something to watch on the TV.

A Folder for Death

He is sometimes there
lounging in my poems about nature and spirit,
love and loss,
gliding his bony finger along
the edge of the page
weighing in on existence and its stoppage,
but today he got his own folder icon on my laptop
because the need to write about him
becomes larger each year
as we step close on life's dance floor.

He takes my wrist, gives me a spin
and though I distract myself
looking at the decorations
the refreshments
the others in the room,
I feel his eyes on me
and understand
he wants to take me home.

Precipice

Interstate conflict, territorial disputes,
transnational terrorism
full blown war,
governments eat at this smorgasbord of political unrest
but never to fullness.

Yemen. Syria. Afghanistan.

Power, control,
domination of souls;
does nothing ever stop
this striving to be on top
of another?

Sudan. Libya.

Decisions, beliefs, ideologies
pile upon humanity
seek allegiance,
while people just look for their next meal,
a job, a warm place to lay,
some form of happiness
joy too large a word,
too fleeting and slippery in this world
of shadows, deception and greed.

Ethiopia. Iraq. Myanmar.

Today another oppressed citizen
throws things in a bag,
pulls on a warm coat, a hat, boots,

grabs a child, a pet
and heads out into the newest line of refugees,
salvaging their life
chased by history, tradition, manipulation,
the wretched legacy of war.

Oh, Ukraine.

Sunset on Mars

My hands want to touch petroglyphs,
pictographs scratched into warm ochre earth,
trace their dry, ancient messages
dug into burnt orange cliffs;
the spirals, the stars, the outlines of people,
feel the greeting of red painted handprints
raised in a hopeful gesture
from neolithic times.

How far we are now from those friendly images
with our world full of rockets, bombs,
a billion guns in a hundred styles.
the exhaust from their dark, smoky language
condemns our failed efforts to reach the beauty of the Sefirot;
Wisdom, Mercy,
Justice, Beauty,
all defined but not absorbed
nor understood in a deep well level
as we lurch in the dark toward forgiveness.

Now, a photo of a sunset on Mars,
the landscape clear, untrod
and what shall we wish for?

Screaming at the Guy at the Transfer Station

I give it my all, you know,
this recycling thing,
been on it since the first Earth Day
picking up, packing out
reusing and using till things are
thread, thin bare.

It was an accident, tossing the rusty lawn chair
its moldy, bug encrusted pink lining well past prime
into the bulky waste, and he yelled at me,
the little guy at the Transfer Station.

"The sign says 'No Metal!'" he yelled.
"No Metal!"

He was right.

(It's a small sign.)

I just went brain dead, and honestly
they make me nervous out there
the men with their scrappy junkyard no-name cat
and their watchful, blank-blue-eyed German Shepherd
fit for a Stephen King novel,
and maybe I was just having a bad day
because I screamed back:

"Next time I'll just leave it all on the side of the road!"

We hollered some more and later I thought
it was anger born of helplessness,
frustration at the bulky waste of our lives
the daily deluge of bad news
uncertain moves
trying to trim it down into something manageable
trying to feel like we are enough.

The Loudest Voice

She is not a screaming, trashy wench,
thinking the loudest voice
wins,
that the first in line is the most
significant,
that her red, white and blue t-shirt and earrings
make her special, more patriotic,
that her aggression is more important
than understanding another.

My lady is patient and strong,
a watchful mother
ready to protect and soothe
though she will fight for right,
put herself on the line
for you
for me
and only ask that we stand with her,
as her broad shoulders
brace against the burdens of injustice.

She is not getting loud in some bar,
slapping her fist on the counter
yelling to get served.
She is not irate that the opinions of others
carry weight
must be considered,
accommodated.

She is rational, thoughtful, intelligent.
She reads, explores.
Knows empathy and compassion are testified
over righteous indignation
over rules and laws

knows it's time to offer real solutions
to all this poverty of body and mind,
if America is to be atoned.

Flags Waving

Colors out
I see you now
pretty poisonous bug
peeling paint house
pot hole slowing us all
down.

Can't pretend it away
or ignore.

How have I lived so long
surrounded by all this
hate?
Can't sweep my steps clean
affairs out of order
mind wandering down dark paths
what ifs, what thens
and I plant my red, white and blue hope
a placard of passion, purity, justice,
look out the window each day
to see if it still stands.

Compounding Disasters

The headline said, "Compounding Disasters,"
and instead of clicking it to life in my inbox
I thought,
"Shouldn't I have that coffee first?"

So, I grabbed a cup and went to my daily horoscope
which mostly rang true, though it said in part:
"You might figure out a way
to handle a problem that has been weighing you down,"

and I knew *that* wasn't true because
I'd already decided to let that problem
die a slow, garden death
you know,
first the frost
then the shriveling from the frost,
then a good garden ghosting till spring
when maybe, you'll set foot on that plot again.

Compounding disasters. Hmm.

I think I'll work on some compounding pleasures:
take a walk, read a book, try a new wine,
pet the cat, make (and eat) a nacho plate,
text a friend (do we still call?)
find that stash of chocolates, down some,
get this crowd to smile and maybe
make some holy laughter.
Let's do a round for Ram Dass, shall we?
Perhaps he'll
hear us in Heaven.

Facebook Buddha/Empty Bowl

Hollow, those words about friendship
and commonality
clanged as they hit the ground.

They clattered about me
and I stood in puzzling wonderment
knowing I'd done nothing to warrant
the pulling of the plug
the cancellation
the shut door,
only held you to account
and no one likes to be called out on their shit;
just ask my husband.

It's easy to wear a Buddha—
earrings, bracelet or T-shirt,
you choose,
easier still to share a post with wise sayings
from renowned ancient teachers
who light the paths of seekers
who then feel they are teachers
graciously sending the wisdom
to uninformed friends like me.

God, give me a Far Side cartoon!
Give me a funny cat video or
an argumentative toddler!
Randy Rainbow!
The Holderness Family!
Scowling Simon Cowell . . . please!

I've seen this shunning before
but thought it was reserved for
bitchy high school girls
or pious church ladies
in cotton blouses and demure skirts.

Always surprised when it comes at me
from the "spiritual" side.
Oh, phony Facebook Buddha,
maybe you should empty your bowl.

Subtle Things

Was the summer too cool?
July and September too abundant with rain?
The clouds of August much to blame?

This fall is muted,
leaves curling green on the branch
then tumbling desiccated
or mottled to a brown peach
ground to sponge on the road.

The lack of candy red, pink and gold
makes me look harder for the beauty I need,
nature's gift before dragging us through another winter.

Chipmunks still scurry,
squirrels bury their cache
pale acorns by the hundreds cover the road, the lawn,
startle drivers when they smack the roof of the car
tiny Zen masters awakening reluctant students.

Meanwhile the air
sweet with decay
promises
something splendid.

Whatever Comes

Sitting with our paper cups of coffee and sweet treats
in the back room of a popular local spot,
we talked of politics, the environment,
our days as teachers and how glad we are
to no longer have to chase down plagiarism
or deal with the A-I factor
now that we're retired,
talked of all the wars, famines and general insanity
around the world
around us
and my friend said,
"I'm almost tired of Mary Oliver.
You know how suddenly
everyone is constantly posting her poems on Facebook.
People sharing Oliver, Rumi, and Frost
in what feels like an almost desperate effort
to find some glimmer,
some goodness to hold on to."

She sighed, suddenly deflated, and at that moment
through the big glass window
I saw the sun,
a blurry golden smear behind a smoky winter cloud
touched her arm,
said, "Look! How beautiful!"
as geese flew south across the sky.

The Phone Rang

I walked into my office as the December dusk
pulled the dark, mauve blanket of itself over its head
and out the window on the rise in the woods
stood three deer.
Noticing me standing in the glow of yellow lamp light
they hesitated, stayed in place,
the largest one holding my gaze.

"The Trinity," I thought,
and how odd that a concept I'd come to question
and one you didn't believe
came to comfort me
as I pressed numbers on the cell phone
to tell everyone,
you'd passed.

*
WINTER

Winter Poems

I

The titmouse puffed against the snow
huddling on the thinnest branch.
A lilac bush is scant shelter in an icy blast.
That bush has grown tall against the house,
but is a reluctant bloom in summer.

II

Everything turned to cupcakes, white and frosted over,
barrels and branches, parapets and stones.
The afternoon moon was high over my shoulder
while the heavy sun dropped toward earth
shooting roses into the tree tops,
shade on all below.

Fallen soldiers on the winter ground,
brown and tangled brambles slung
purple shadows across the frozen blanket.
All still, silent, as the mother's winter breath
whispered her message onto my cheeks.

Snow Globe

Last night in bed I could feel it
pushing all around me,
down from the roof and from
the sides of the sky—
all that snow.
Pounds of it, terrorizing
all of us, birds, squirrels, deer.
(Where are the poor deer?)

Heavy, cold accusation
we struggle against it,
bravely scraping and digging our way out
piling it ever higher as
we wander in this snow globe
this beautiful treachery,
shaking ourselves to sun and spring.

Solstice Moon

Lavender-pink morning moon
flies past the solstice night.
Four-hundred-year winter night,
eclipsed and unseen by dreamers.

Lovely, full, unconditional moon,
touching us together
when we cannot.
Beaming love into the dark places,
reflecting hope.

Bear

Gold lays in the soul,
heavy
hard to carry
exhaustion putting one to sleep on winter days.
The worth of it too dear,
the responsibility
makes rising difficult.

Accounts to be paid, squared.
Affairs to be sorted out,
rectified, confirmed.

So, I am a bear,
sleeping on the sofa
holding ingots
waiting for birds and light
to surround my bulk,
animate me into spring.

Favorite Goddess

Cynthia waxes,
manages her money
shops off season for the children's clothes
stretches the meat with casseroles
smiles at her husband.

Selene wanes,
lights small candles
bundles the baby, the grandmother,
cocooning them in blankets woven for beauty,
hums to herself.

Like Hecate at the crossroads a woman waits for grain,
for water, the line winding and wide like the Nile
life pressing against her hip,
laying gentle in her tired hand.

Beyond, in the pitch and quiet of space,
Artemis flies, seeking herself in beaming moonlight,
hunting a discovery for men on a mission
holding no answers
for Earth's struggling, steadfast daughters.

Tombs

Rebekah

Polly

Silence

Obadiah Stone

have disintegrated underground
their colonial bones
released into the earth
their pine boxes dissolved
and the messages sent
are clear
though the carved words on their headstones
are lost to the rain and the wind
softening back into themselves,
the granite unable to hold them.

                The messages say:
                Look! Listen! Act!

Endure your lot as we did
we who died in fire and war,
in cold,
from exhaustion,
we who buried these babies
with comfortless faith
placing small stones above their heads,
something solid in this world of waves and uncertainty.

We who were slaves and immigrants
buried together beneath this tree shout at you.
Even the rich laying in sturdy mausoleums
repeat,

"No time."
"No time for regret."

Cellophane

All that philosophy
all that time
and
all that time
                                      alone
created insight
twin sight

your shoes on my feet
my feet on your path
and I became wiser,
leaned in
experienced the other
got a handle on things;
the why, the when, the how.

Warnings were given:
"Be careful! It might be too much!"
"You might regret it, all that understanding,"
but diamond translucence
cellophane hearts and clear-corridor eyes
gave me more power than Eve,
a treasure map placed in my hands
for peace and protection.

Asymmetry

We have, we have not.
We see, we are confused.
We hear, we misunderstand.
What's clear in the wreckage of war
is that some things can't be put back
together;
shredded paper
smashed porcelain
bones, bones, bones
of the dead,
families missing their pieces,
while sane explanations of
"strategies" for "winning"
explode like bombs in our ears
leaving a hollow ring.

"There has been an asymmetrical response,"
one reporter said,
stepping out on the ledge of his career,
and his honest statement almost felt
like hope,
which has run out for tens of thousands,
and my carefully gleaned philosophy
that all things work for good
is a hard fit these days
a shrunken sweater that won't go over my head
as I hear the world call "peace," "peace," "peace,"
cease the fire,
stop the killing,
stop killing children.

O Holy Night

A quiet night, a holy night,
(aren't they all holy?)
a time to settle
meditate
sing.

Many will pray this Christmas,
pray harder than before
for War's children everywhere
especially for the people of Palestine
children of the desert,
their ancient history recorded, retold,
the most famous story
reenacted around the world for centuries;
generations of angels, donkeys, shepherds and stars
standing in chancels and sanctuaries
as a narrator recited:
"Then the angel said to them, 'Do not be afraid, for behold,
I bring you good tidings of great joy which will be to all people.'"

There is no joy in Palestine
no celebration allowed through this ruptured wound
as the people run from bombs,
search for food, water, shelter,
so many holy families
trying to hear the angel sing.

The Tide

Led here by hope, lack, lust
our ancestors pulled roots
sailed away,
we live in their wake
trying to reshape
events not of our making
but now of our surroundings.

The wider world shouts across mountains and seas
and we distract from attacks
our handprints on many troubles,
others, we didn't start;
try to numb a bit
fashion an outcome
fit to live with
while the Rot of Ages
presses in
tide rises,
we try to stem
keep the dike from bursting
look at each other and say,
"Hold, hold."

Weather Report

Like one long November
this winter with no snow
(fun to take a year off—
no shoveling, sanding, slipping,
minus ice is nice),
but the ashen gray, grayness
of old blanket in the sky
tamps down the damper
clamps us champs
we're pale and pasty
can't eat enough vitamins
drink enough sunny juice-shine
to balance out all this sog & bog
and really

isn't "getting away with it"
supposed to feel better
than this?

Sunday at Rusty's

Mild for February after a day's arctic blast,
we head down to the beach
an hour plus drive
getting out of the house,
away from who we sometimes are together
now that the kids are gone and there is
so much of us to deal with.

We walk Sachuest Point, a preserve,
and do see a pheasant with its bright white ring
three deer grazing on a hill
hear a nascent bird repeat her call
imagine Algonquians roaming the cliffs.

We climb the slate rock remnants of Pangea,
gift from the three-pronged fissure
that pushed Paleozoic continents apart,
gaze at the pale quartz bluffs below
the green-gray churning ocean
notice the sun's rays pushing against the gauzy sky
sense our part in the play.

Later, over fish and chips
in a dive bar you claimed had a 5-star rating
we sat at a table apart from the regulars
sons and daughters of fishermen, deckhands,
barmaids, housekeepers.
Some laughed loudly at jokes we couldn't hear
some watched the game
others stared only at the drink before them
perhaps, like me, pondering
all the steps of life leading us to this place,
wondering where next our feet will fall.

Bellerophon's Downfall

Sometimes I suspect
God might not be happy with me
since I cannot seem to drop
my sarcastic, irreverent side
because sometimes it gets a laugh.

Landscaping my life
trying to reconnect with that soft, gentle part of myself
I lifted rocks, transplanted trees, pulled weeds
raked and trimmed trying to make things fit like before,
before the damage,
before the humiliation,
before I toughened up.

Raised by warm women's hands
and soft, aproned bodies that hugged and soothed,
watchful dads, a neighborhood of them,
caring adults,
I was never abused
until later.

Lucky me.

Sometimes I am mean.
Mostly on the inside,
muttering comments to myself,
occasionally a snide aside escapes;
don't mean any of it, just blowing steam,
releasing the hurt.
I am trying still to love this hard world
and her crabby, salty, stroppy people.

Fighting chimeras with my emails and Tweets,
my small donations, reaching for righteousness,
and I worry that like Bellerophon, I will be thrown from my horse,

God sending a gadfly to bite me as I aim my sights on Heaven,
not good enough to make the cut,
dropped back down to the hard earth of my life.

I mean, that's what I think
sometimes.

The Burning of Old Love

Unwise to let it fester,
spiral notebooks crammed with
old feelings
revealing too much pain
too much loss
my hasty cursive running on the lines,
an arroyo of emotion.

It had to be released, I know,
but it's a decade later
and some decent poems
now sit in books,
on the net,
shared on stage,
time now to tear the pages out
throw them in the woodstove,
let some of the secrets turn to unpublished ash.

Guess You Forgot

Gazing at tiny fingers, unused feet,
watching first bites, first walks, first words;
in the photos you look proud.

I guess you forgot.

Sunday afternoons chasing three-year-old me
around the hedge in front of that little rental house
till I screamed with joy
felt like I had to pee
snapping my picture as I gasped for breath,
all the adults laughing.

I guess you forgot.

Rare Saturdays after clothes shopping with Mom
we'd come home and do a "fashion show"
just for you, letting you admire our new outfits,
you always looked pleased.

I guess you forgot.

Guess you forgot all that love
that turned to a bitter river
running from your mouth,
sour sayings full of defeat and loss.
It wasn't because of me.
I did everything for your praise, your respect,
but I guess you forgot.

February Sun

That nail is going to rip
again
in the same place,
reminding me how little
control I have
over a great many things
in my battle to curb nature.

This month has been long
testing my patience
like a midnight drum
like a mad songbird
and there are two weeks to go.

"I put on many clothes,"
the meaning of February in ancient Japanese:
Kisaragi,
distinct from the rest of the winter.

Still, the word doesn't tell all;
doesn't explain
how worn down one can feel
after so many months of cold, gray, wet limitation.

But today the sun is out,
and the snow cap on creation is bright and clean.
Helios and Kalinda extend their golden arms
and I will not refuse their invitation
to walk in the world.

This View

Could there be anything better
than this view out my bedroom window?
Winter edging away,
withered leaves clinging
deflated like old peaches,
shuddering in the breeze?

From this chair only one-third
of the trunks are visible;
one's base,
the other's middle,
shadows altering.
A newcomer would not know
how stalwart and strong,
optimistic and reaching they are.

A bit of hillside is discernable too,
brambly branches poking through
a layer of hard crunch snow
still tight on the ground,
a frosty, fitted sheet of white.
A newcomer would not know
the size of the hill,
nor how the children used to run its length,
and laugh among these precious trees.

From the Dark

A voice from the dark
speaks quietly to the living light,
a soft, devastated voice
without tears or trembling
because the woman of this voice
has seen too much
traveling through this beast's belly
for more than a year
and now knows what
humankind can do
to children
to hospitals full of elderly, ill
and injured people,
to entire towns,
knows the outcome of bombs
the smell of death and garbage.
"The world is complicit in this.
No one must be silent in this," she states.

She expects nothing now,
after her year of messages
cast upon the online sea,
her Emmy, her fame,
but wishes the world would march
to the borders of Gaza,
call out, shout, pray
make a presence that would
stop the madness.
"What next?" Bisan asks, "what next?"

Bisan Owda is a young journalist in Gaza who created travel videos before the war. She received an Emmy and a Peabody award for covering her experience of the events in her country after the atrocities of October 7th, 2023.

Reclamation

Old stone steps vanish from view year by year
vines and ferns strangling them in slow determination
the house already turned to earth,
but the stones, though hidden, remain fixed
like how bright summer light overtakes spring's delicate tinge
or how fall grabs the bolder greens
splashing them leaf by leaf with jewel tones of
vermillion, aubergine, aurelian,
how winter withers that beauty in its own strong grip,
each season reclaiming its place.

Hearts too, can be reclaimed,
like the Lycaenidae of England,
velvety blue butterflies
nearly lost in the depleted meadowlands
reemerging with care,
with tending,
with desire for another chance at love.

The Idea of It

Odd beauties surround me,
like the way light changes and chases the day
passing along all the objects of the world
plashing wall shadows in odd places,
casting itself into bathroom mirrors
then reflecting that brilliance onto walls,
bouncing off jewelry abandoned on countertops
leaving behind rainbow fragments and hope.

Green and golden eyed cats,
the whole idea of cats—
Egyptian cats, Salem cats,
silly Felix and theatrical Grizelda
howling her memories at the moon;
corduroy and its soft recollections,
how it comforts me
returning me to a time before pain;
tin ceilings preserved in old Victorian buildings
and humble restaurants,
the surprise of looking up to find this history
protecting me.

That Paul and Ringo call each other
twice a month, proving some friendships do last;
that perfect top swirl on a Dairy Queen soft serve cone,
the saccharine taste on my tongue,
the glow from our house
when we've remembered
to leave the light on.

Toward the Horizon

A slant of winter sunlight tinged the trees
cast its rose gold stream across our patch of woods
the beam low in the morning sky
a searchlight along the cold ground
landing on leaves faded to peach
everything awash in done, over, finished,
and the brown of everything made me wish
for the missing snow, the ice,
the normalcy of January past
when folded coverlets pressed the sleeping soil
a shimmer of white over all the dead and waiting,
a season to be counted on.

Now, I count on nothing,
the weather a carnival pendulum ride,
political alliances shifting,
economies surfing on the Covid waves.
I mask up,
keep my distance
destroy a lifetime of work breaking through
feelings that kept me apart,
my authentic self now encouraged to
go back inside and hide,
but the birds have flown to the horizon,
summoning the dawn,
and their song is a key unlocking despair.
Listen! They are singing now.

*
S
P
R
I
N
G

Rite of Spring

Our yard sits in shadow,
sliced into a second growth forest
a fortress of thin, tall trees surrounds the house
letting winter linger at the edges during March and April.

It is New England, after all.

Warming trends and balmy Midwestern winds
will blow up to the front door
melting snow enough to see the mashed grass,
make visible the nascent buds on bushes and trees.
Skunk cabbage appears beside the brook
and the tips of July's day lilies push through the rocky flower bed;
these things can be counted on.

But near the driveway each year
a crescent of snow and gravel refuse a natural thaw.
This icy crust clings together
a lump of false conclusion,
taunting me.

Left with only violence
I take up the shovel
stab the icy tumor till it comes apart,
kick the rest with my boot and
make certain that spring will come.

Dream in March

The day was raw and wet and there was little comfort being indoors when everyone felt like going home and sitting on the couch, but we kept our forced smiles, and after some minutes of pleasantries and weak jokes we went silent.

The rain kept coming; a third day of rain. At noon the drops widened, pelted down onto the sad remnants of last summer's garden, a long dead affair. We decided it was a "wintry mix," made more lame jokes, laughed a bit, then got back to work. No games today. No funny stuff. We just want the thing to end— the school year and the terrible weather. We just want warm sand, cool drinks and sunsets of blue flame and fire.

We want to put away the beat-up books, stack the chairs, and not come back into this blue cement room with all the metal, and the fake wood trim, stop hearing the buzzers that pierce our ears every forty-two minutes; buzzers that give extra bursts of nail—in—the—brain noise at lunch time in intervals of twenty.

We want to stay in bed and hear a bird sing outside our window, or sit with our 3 p.m. snacks on the back deck, watching shadows of leaf and limb paint pictures across the boards. We want to walk barefoot everywhere, anywhere we choose, and not care if we forget our jackets at home because it's warm, and we don't need them.

We want all those things. Simple things, really, and we will get them, if we can just survive the raw.

Little League Moms

The games could get heated
and parents of naturally athletic boys,
the Little League All-Stars,
cliqued together in the stands
the rest of us sheepishly sitting away
hoping our kid wouldn't be the one
to make the last out, lose the game.

One night the mom of the best player
lost her mind
started yelling at the kids on our team
who were striking out,
dropping balls.

At first, we didn't get it,
that her calls of "Rag arm!"
and "You can't hit a barn door!"
were aimed at her son's own teammates,
then silently
we second-tier moms
got up
took seats surrounding her
and enforced the code of conduct.

Future Perfect

You will have arrived.
We will have had our dinner and gone dancing.
She will have returned home for a visit;
perhaps she will have decided
to stay—
to remain,
permanently.

We will have stopped fighting.
We will have sorted out the finances.
You will have received word
that the vacation was approved.

He will have learned
that the lump was really
nothing.
We will have discovered the new beer,
the latest band,
the best way to forgive.

Intention

One sound
bound
by unseen chords
we act
and interact
in disharmony
looking for a melody we can play,
a song
to make sense of suffering.

Plants thrive
children grow wise
in 4/4 time,
their vibrancy a consolation.

Emoto found messages in the water
snapped frozen emotions
liquid reactions to suggestions of love, hate,
friendship, loneliness,
his photos of the sad patterns of accosted droplets
so different from praised water.

We are water.

We know it's true:
praise lifts,
criticism rips
and some damage is done without sound;
the profound condemnation of silence.

We are water.
Speak kindly, send solace.

Gratitude

So, years went by
lives were led
you stayed in town
I moved away
and my last memory of you is
a spring break visit to your apartment.

You had the second baby
the toddler ran about
and you were busy and attentive to those little ones,
but the place was dark and small and all the light
was outside
and all the happy laughter was also
outside,
and I remember feeling grateful
as I drove away in my mother's car.

Your MG

Summer?
Spring!
1977 and young,
top down on that red MG—
you, driving me home.

And I laughed out loud,
asked,
"Do you ever feel
like nothing could ever get you?"

Because I felt that good.

Of course, after a bit of a pause
you told me

"No."

That is the cost of war.

When I Think of Utah

. . . it's that long road
cutting through worn stone cliffs,
beige, rust and ginger
an eon of endurance
running along both sides of the highway
shimmering in spring heat,
a promise
a mirage
as we headed to Seattle toward a new life
a big adventure
bigger than the mountains we crossed
through Montana, Wyoming.

Though we did end up in the green Northwest
with cool, clean air, mountains abounding
at night we traveled to swampy Vietnam
your demons digging themselves out of buried memories
completely freed by the end of our first year of marriage
chasing me into a new life.

Now, your road has taken you back to Utah,
a third wife receiving gifts
brought by time and therapy
while sometimes I'm still searching the delta for you.

Moonlight Becomes Her

I wanted to be your moon,
reflect your glowing golden light back to you
out to everyone,
let them see your audacious wonder!

The striking alabaster moon in the obsidian sky
absorbs all attention till clouds and cold come
reminding us how we really love the day,
the feel of feet on warm silky sand,
backs resting against sun-soaked benches
succumbing to those comfortable rays
delicious, a narcotic of letting go
eyes forced to close, doze under its irrefutable power.

I wanted to be your moon,
dazzled as I was
not knowing I could be my own star,
my own burning luminary.

When violence erupted from you
I left,
scared though I was
certain only that
you.   would not.   hit me.

It was enough motivation.

Later I learned most women stay.

I could have been the best moon,
your Magdalene, your Jeanne, your queen,

but life pushed me out onto my own sun-lit stage,
made me a headliner.
For years I felt betrayed
because
I was such a good moon,
but Sol called, and I couldn't say no.

If You Were Mine

If you were mine there would be
bills to pay
appointments to keep
relations to appease
and meals to get hot and on time to the table.

We would argue about the finances
who would give the baby her bath
why we needed to visit your mother one more time,
and I would be angry at you
for not knowing
the days of the children's dentist appointments,
the size of their shoes.

If you were mine
we would have to paint the living room
together
blame each other for the spills on the carpet,
the poor color choice.
We would plan vacations,
fight over the packing
and the way things were to be put
into the car.

If you were mine,
you would one day
start leaving your clothes
poking out of all your drawers
just to upset me, and I would
withhold my affections
until the isolation felt normal,
if ever you were mine.

Real Heart

Because I had a real heart
I understood for too long
accepted too much
missed some clues.

Because I had a real heart
wounds went deep
words meant more
sounds scratched and bit.

Because I had a real heart
it was layered over for protection
with durable material
strong as steel
keeping out debris, rain, wind,
staying cold
preserving the insides
like a refrigerator.

But it's not a self-defrosting fridge.
It's an old-fashioned heart.
Bring the hot water, a towel,
the knife to chip the ice.
It might take an hour.

Bring a book.

Honorable Mention

Hour hand on the eight
probably
can't be sure
but this late in life
it might be
good enough
to get an "honorable mention,"
be told that what you did
almost rose to the level of
excellence
but for those few bad choices,
that anger you still carry
like a favorite handbag,
the few you decided
to freeze out
because you couldn't
keep the door of your
heart
your battered heart
open enough
to let them back in.

Nice try, no cigar
but still,
an honorable mention.

Dent-de-lion

The swirl of the world
its flora and fauna
brings nothing closer to truth
than the dent-de-lion.

Sunshine burst
a moon and stars
a map of the cosmos
in seed and stem.

Hold in your hand its lions' teeth
to renew you in spring,
courage to continue
spread along every river,
every lawn.
Viewed from above, its yellow life expired
it is snowflake,
a puff-ball parachute
flying sparks of hope.

Gaze again, see
a crisscross puzzle
a mandala
hope, healing, resilience in each sacred stitch.

Searching

I type "Is Bisan" in the search bar,
and the next two words appear automatically
with their furtive question mark, "still alive?"

Bisan, a Palestinian journalist, popped into my Facebook feed
one morning during this latest Mideast roil,
her fresh, round face full of promise
her troubled brown eyes alert as she posted
cell phone videos of the wreckage of Palestine,
the slaughter of the people.
The videos are raw, wound the eyes, sear the soul.
She posts each time she must flee, relocate,
so many displacements now she's lost count.
One day she shows us her favorite flower
the passionate poppy, *Hannoun,* red, alive
pushing forth in the spring air,
another day she videos a small boy selling homemade potato chips.
"Delicious, tasty!" she says, almost smiling,
boys flying kites on the beach behind her.
These moments are her sustenance
as she shares pictures of her home in the Gaza ruins,
a video of the day a bomb at Al-Shifa hospital just missed her
by two minutes,
her refugee life in Rafah,
stories of others spit out by this war
hundreds of thousands with no safe place to go,
their way home stalled, like the peace talks.

Bisan is 25.
She is forthright, emotional, outraged,

bewildered.
She wonders where is help? Why is this allowed to go on?
Seven months now.

She looks into the phone's lens. Begs,
"Don't get used to
what is happening in Gaza!"
She is searching for rationality, for assistance.
I will keep searching for her,
pray she can send more videos of children flying their kites,
sending up wishes,
pray that those wishes get answered.

Mercy

Baseball season upon us
new uniforms bought
grass groomed
coaches ready for the field
hungry to shape those players into contenders,
forge teams who can rally against rivals.

But sometimes you get outdone
by strength
size
dumb luck.
Sometimes you strike out.

Sometimes, a team needs mercy.

Wish the world was more like baseball,
not too much grandstanding
egos in check
working together
shaking hands with opponents
umpires calling "Mercy"
when enough is enough,
the winning already done.

Watching Animal Rescue Videos

A man opens his kitchen door, finds a tiny fawn waiting.
The fawn makes no sound, just stares sweetly
till the man steps out,
follows it to a patch of woods, her father trapped
his 12—point antlers wrapped around a tree trunk.
Sawed free, the muscular buck runs off.
Next morning, the buck is discovered waiting by the door,
his intense gaze a silent thank you.

There is more.
A sea turtle returns with a jelly fish to share
with a diver who cut it free from plastic bindings.
The turtle nibbles the gelatinous treat while the diver pretends,
looks in the turtle's eyes;
a dolphin who returned to a pier for four days, on the last day
bringing a beach ball to toss with his new friend;
a golden fox who brings her kits, shows them off to the man who
pulled her from a car grill, took her to a vet.

Then, a final video. A huge eagle stands still in the road.
Traffic stops.
A woman gets out, and with another driver
they gather him in her faded blue rain coat
and she carries him like a toddler, puts him in her car.
Time lapse, and we see another vet heal the eagle's brokenness;
a bandaged wing
salve for a head wound
eye drops.

Time lapse again and
and this now restored symbol is freed at some football stadium,
soars over the heads of hundreds
sweet release
and I am weeping for all we do,
for all we lose,
for all we wish to be.

Nothing Left but to Be a Shaman

Signed the petitions
went to the town meetings
sent the voter cards, money,
encouraging words.

Held hands at the rallies
raised signs
raised hell
called the congressmen
the representatives
the mayor
the selectmen
asked them
to protect our land, our water,
our animals.

Wrote the letters
made the posts
read the books
watched the documentaries
attended the hearings.

Not much is moving.

Guess all that's left
is to be
a shaman,
put my power into kindness,
be helpful, soft,
speak my heart-won
hard-won
truth,

hold it out like an ageless apple,
put on a purple shirt
some quiet shoes,
sit around a fire

sending smoky messages to the stars
release all my wishes into the vast
deep of space,
wait for an ancient answer.

A Burst of Sunshine

A wave went round the world this week,
congratulations for tapping into star power,
but others did it first
blending us into something new,
their gravitational pull undeniable
as we crashed into orbits without consent
no way to resist such talent and charm
and we were changed,
the way the sun's gravity compresses hydrogen atoms,
fuses them into helium
the complete transformation
a burst of irrepressible energy;
we became light!

Ah, who can forget their first love?

About the Author

Karen Warinsky lives in Connecticut and began publishing poetry in 2011. A finalist of the Montreal International Poetry Contest (2013) and a Best of the Net Nominee (2023), she received First Place from the Ekphrastic Poetry Trust (2024) for her poem "Mirage." She has read in many online open mics including Rattlecast, Wednesday Night Poetry, and Ó Bhéal; is a frequent featured poet in Connecticut and Massachusetts at various venues; and coordinates poetry readings under the name Poets at Large in Connecticut and Massachusetts.

Her work appears in several anthologies including *Joy Interrupted: a journal of motherhood and loss* (Fat Daddy Publishing, 2012), *Global Poetry Anthology* (Véhicule Press, 2013), *Nuclear Impact: Broken Atoms in Our Hands* (Shabda Press, 2017), *Mizmor Anthology* (2019), *Honoring Nature* (Human Error Publishing, 2021), and *New Generation Beats 2022 Anthology* (National Beat Poetry Foundation, Inc. 2022). As well, her work appears in the books *Dear Nana* (Pegasus Books, 2015) and *Ms. Aligned 4, Coming of Age* (Ms. Aligned Books, et. al. 2023).

Her poems also appear in dozens of journals, e-zines, and online sites, including *Blue Heron, Circumference, Consilience, The New Verse News, The Naugatuck River Review, Silkworm, Light,* and *Wordpeace*. Her work has also been published in *Worcester Magazine* and *The Rambler* newspaper.

Warinsky has three poetry collections: *Gold in Autumn* (Human Error Publishing, 2020), *Sunrise Ruby* (Human Error Publishing, 2022) and *Dining with War* (Alien Buddha Press, 2023).

Find out more at:
Website: karenwarinskypoetry.wordpress.com
Instagram: @karenw.21

www.ingramcontent.com/pod-product-compliance
Lightning Source LLC
Chambersburg PA
CBHW060839190426
43197CB00040B/2687